On the Farm

Chickens

Hens, Roosters, and Chicks

Lorijo Metz

PowerKiDS press
New York

To my fellow hens in the Caribou Coop: Kathleen, Diana, and Amy

Published in 2011 by The Rosen Publishing Group, Inc.
29 East 21st Street, New York, NY 10010

First Edition

Editor: Amelie von Zumbusch
Book Design: Greg Tucker
Photo Researcher: Jessica Gerweck

Photo Credits: Cover, pp. 4, 6, 7, 8, 9 (top), 11, 12, 13, 14, 15, 16, 18, 20, 21 Shutterstock.com; p. 5 Timothy Laman/Getty Images; p. 9 (bottom) © www.iStockphoto.com/Stephan Westcott; p. 10 Peter Anderson/Getty Images; p. 17 MoMo Productions/Getty Images; p. 19 Karin Dreyer/Getty Images; p. 22 Jean Michel Foujols/Getty Images.

Library of Congress Cataloging-in-Publication Data

Metz, Lorijo.
Chickens : hens, roosters, and chicks / Lorijo Metz. — 1st ed.
p. cm. — (On the farm)
Includes index.
ISBN 978-1-4488-0691-1 (library binding) — ISBN 978-1-4488-1343-8 (pbk.) — ISBN 978-1-4488-1344-5 (6-pack)
1. Chickens—Juvenile literature. I. Title. II. Series: Metz, Lorijo. On the farm.
SF487.5.M48 2011
636.5—dc22

2010006019

Manufactured in the United States of America

CPSIA Compliance Information: Batch #WS10PK: For Further Information contact Rosen Publishing, New York, New York at 1-800-237-9932

Contents

Meet the Chicken

Which came first, the chicken or the egg? We may never know, but chickens are interesting birds! They can fly, but not very far or very high. They run fast, though. Chickens can run about 9 miles per hour (14 km/h). Farmers

This mother chicken is watching over a group of fluffy chicks. A group of chicks is often known as a brood.

who raise chickens are called **poultry** farmers. Most chickens are raised for their eggs and meat. Male chickens are called roosters. Female chickens are called hens. Baby chickens are called chicks.

Red jungle fowl, such as this rooster, are members of the pheasant family. As you can see, red jungle fowl roosters are very colorful.

Domesticated chickens came from wild chickens called red jungle fowl. Red jungle fowl still live in parts of Asia today. Scientists think that people in India and Southeast Asia likely began keeping chickens about 7,000 years ago.

What Do Chickens Look Like?

Roosters, such as the one on the left here, always have spurs. Hens sometimes have spurs, too, but that is more uncommon.

As all birds do, chickens have feathers and two wings. Chickens also have pointy beaks and claws for feet. Chicken claws are good for **scratching** in dirt and holding on to **perches**. Most chicken claws have four toes. Roosters also have **spurs**.

One thing that makes chickens different from most other birds is that they have **wattles** and combs. A comb is the red crown

Farm Facts

How can you tell a rooster from a hen? Roosters are generally larger and have brighter, more colorful feathers. They also have larger, brighter wattles and combs.

The chicken on the left is a rooster, while the one on the right is a hen. You can easily see the male's bigger comb and wattles.

on the top of a chicken's head. Combs come in different shapes. Some of these shapes are called strawberry, buttercup, and pea. Wattles are two red parts that hang beneath a chicken's chin. Wattles help chickens keep cool.

Chicken Breeds

There are many chicken **breeds**. Most of the eggs in stores come from standard chicken breeds, such as Rhode Island reds and Sussex chickens. Standard chickens most often weigh between 4 and 7 pounds (2–3 kg). The heaviest chicken ever recorded was a white Sully. It weighed 22 pounds (10 kg).

Buff Orpingtons, such as this young chicken, are raised for both meat and eggs.

Bantam chickens, known as banties, generally weigh 1 to 2 pounds (.5–1 kg).

This rooster is a Plymouth Rock rooster. Many Plymouth Rock chickens are barred, or striped, as this rooster is.

Though they lay smaller eggs, people like raising banties because they require less space. They also tend to be calmer. Silkie banties are known as the lap kittens of the chicken world. They have fluffy, silklike feathers. Seramas are one of the world's smallest chicken breeds. They weigh only .5 pound (227 g).

Silkie bantams, such as this chicken, are covered in soft feathers. They even have feathers on their legs!

From Chicks to Chickens

Like all baby birds, chicks **hatch** from eggs. A hen lays 1 egg each day until she has about 10 eggs. This is called a clutch. The hen sits on her eggs in a nest of feathers and straw. She turns the eggs several times a day to keep them warm.

A mother hen's body heat and soft feathers keep her eggs warm.

After three weeks, chicks begin to hatch. Chicks hatch by using their egg teeth. These are sharp bumps on the tops of their beaks. They tap their shells until

Newly hatched chicks, such as these, are born with soft feathers called down. As they grow older, their adult feathers will grow in.

they break. For the first five months, chicks stay with their mothers. Mother hens teach their chicks what to eat. At night, hens keep their chicks safe under their wings.

Mother hens often help their chicks find food. When a hen finds food, she will make noises to let her chicks know.

What Do Chickens Eat?

Chickens scratch and peck to find food. They eat everything from plants and seeds to insects and worms. They even eat dirt and stones!

On a small farm, such as this one, chickens often scratch in the barnyard to find food.

Farmers feed chickens special food, called mash, from **troughs**. They make sure chickens have enough clean water, too.

Chickens do not have teeth, so they swallow their food whole. At first, a chicken's food is stored in a pouch, called a crop, in its throat. The food then makes its way to the chicken's stomach. There, it mixes with juices that help break it down. Finally, the food enters the chicken's **gizzard**. There, it is ground up with the help of dirt and stones that the chicken has eaten.

This boy is feeding the chicks on his family's farm. Chicks on farms are generally fed a special kind of food, known as starter crumbles.

How Do Chickens Live?

Chickens like to live in small groups, called flocks. One rooster looks after several hens. The birds spend much of the day outside eating and taking dust baths. Dust baths help chickens stay cool. They also remove insects and dirt from their skin. Chickens also use their beaks to preen, or clean, their feathers.

Here, you can see a flock of chickens. The rooster is the large, white bird in the middle.

These chickens are climbing up a ladder into their chicken coop for the night. Chicken coops often have ladders.

Chickens do not see well at night. To keep safe, they sleep in houses called chicken coops. At night they roost, or sleep standing up. They hold on to perches with their feet.

The chickens in a flock have a pecking order. This means that there is a set order of which chickens boss around which other chickens.

Farm Facts

Some chickens raised on larger farms never go outside. They live in large houses with thousands of chickens. Machines clean the cages and give the chickens food and water.

Chickens Raised for Meat

People around the world eat chicken. In the last few years, people have started eating even more chicken. Most people like the taste of chicken. Many also like that chicken meat is low in fat. It is a great source of **protein**, too.

Roast chicken, seen here, is another well-liked way to prepare a chicken.

There are thousands of ways to cook chicken, from American fried chicken to Indian tandoori chicken. One of the best-known chicken dishes is chicken soup. As far back as ancient Egypt, people ate chicken soup when they had colds.

Today, much of the chicken in stores comes from Cornish chickens. Cornish chickens grow quickly. Farmers also cross Cornish chickens with other breeds to produce meat chickens.

This boy is eating fried chicken. There are many different ways to cook fried chicken.

Chicken Eggs

This boy is breaking an egg into his mixing bowl while making a cake. Most cakes and cookies have eggs in them.

People all over the world eat eggs, too. Some people eat eggs boiled, scrambled, or fried. There are also thousands of dishes, from pancakes to cookies to egg foo yong, that use eggs.

A hen can lay 180 to 320 eggs each year. Most chickens lay brown or white eggs. Some breeds lay green or blue eggs, though! To lay eggs, hens need a certain amount of daylight. In fall and winter, when there is less

Farm Facts

Hens do not need roosters to lay eggs, only to have eggs turn into chicks. The eggs you buy in the store cannot turn into baby chicks.

This girl and her mother have gathered a bowl of eggs that were laid by the hens on their farm. Freshly laid eggs taste extra good!

daylight, hens lay fewer eggs. In the spring, egg **production** goes up again as the days lengthen. To keep their hens laying, farmers must gather the eggs every day.

Free-Range and Factory-Farm Chickens

Many people argue that the meat and eggs from free-range chickens, such as these ones, taste better because they lead healthier lives.

On some farms, chickens spend their days outside. They walk around the farmyard in search of food. Farmers call chickens raised this way free-range chickens. These chickens often live on farms that also raise other kinds of animals.

Today, though, poultry farming has become a big business. Many chickens are raised on huge farms called factory farms. These chickens spend their whole lives inside with thousands of other

Farm Facts

Free-range chickens most often live for six to eight years. Chickens raised in factory farms generally live for two to three years.

These egg-laying chickens live on a large factory farm. Factory-farm chickens produce millions of eggs every year.

chickens. Factory-farm chickens are raised to grow quickly and produce lots of eggs. In the United States, there are more than 200 companies with flocks numbering 75,000 chickens or more.

Beyond Meat and Eggs

While chickens supply us with meat and eggs, their feathers are also useful. Scientists have found ways to use chicken feathers to make **environmentally friendly** plastics. You may soon see this plastic used for everything from candy wrappers to flowerpots.

These girls have a pet chicken. Chickens make good pets. They are friendly and fun to watch.

People are also using feathers to make new types of environmentally friendly **fabrics**. In the future, it seems that people will not only eat chickens, they will wear them as well!